# Frenchie Hart

## A Poetic Memoir

Thank you for
sharing my
journey! ♡
Jen

***A note from the author:***

***Thank you for sharing my journey***

***Please remember self-love is the greatest love.***

With appreciation:
Please share your thoughts and feelings
frenchiehart@gmail.com

To purchase additional copies of this book email
frenchiehart@gmail.com


Written between 2008 and 2015
Frenchie Hart is registered with the Library of Congress,
TXu002081095; effective date December 29, 2017
ISBN: 978-0-578-61328-4

The Mind is its own place

And in itself can make a heaven of hell

A hell of heaven

~ John Milton ~

**This Book is dedicated to:**

**Paul Mirabile**

Because he said I could and should.

Please - Always Smile, Laugh and Forever Giggle

Thank you, "Pilot Bill" Hagan for introducing us.

**Acknowledgments:**

Thank you to those who have sacrificed their hearts, minds, bodies and souls. Without emotional torment we never grow. I thank you and myself for our so-called "failures", without them I would have not won the battle in my head or the war in my heart.

Thank you to the one I continue to love…..you know who you are. - *ME*

For my one true love - I know you are out there looking for me. Until the day comes when we meet, please know I am already thankful that you want to share your life with me. I look forward to the new chapters we will write together. May are days ahead be blessed with peace, love and happiness.

Thank you to my dearest friend, and lifetime partner in crime, Wendy Burtnick. I truly appreciate your patience, your time, and willingness to edit my book. I hope you found yourself at the wine store or the coffee shop during this process and not on the phone scheduling therapy appointments! With your help, I feel, I have mastered not only the use of the comma but also a proactive use of my thoughts! Thank you! XO

Thank you to the Broad Axe Tavern in Blue Bell, PA, for giving me a place of refuge and sanctuary.

~ For none of this would be possible ~

**Decide**

Do you think we are stuck somewhere between Love and Good-bye?

Are we running on auto pilot?

Are we growing?

Progressing?

Are we moving backwards to move forward? Have we lost ourselves and each other ….again?

Have we passed each other, once more, like two ships passing in the night?

Have we completed our cycle?

Where are we going? And are we going there together?

Are we running parallel with each other? Will we find out in the end our separate paths have brought us to separate ends?

My days are consumed with thoughts of you- us- them. It's as if I don't have any other purpose in life right now, except to think – yet thinking only gets one so far

Actions are needed.

A voice needs to be heard

Something or someone needs to give

A plan – not an attack

Success not Failure

One day at a time....everyday...but for how long? How long is too long? How long?

And yet- is it enough

Patience... Love... Peace?

Happiness

Temptations or Frustrations

Were we ever really "real" to begin with?

Have we changed?  Or have our expectations changed? Maybe nothing has changed at all?

Running in circles

I think we *know* the truth, we just can't *see* it.

We are still entranced by the pendulum we have put into motion

It is consistent

Reliable, Secure, Predictable

Heavy and swings from one extreme to the other

Regulating our somewhere in between

Love or Good –bye

Decide.

**Say it with a Smile and Follow it with a Laugh**

There is something I need to tell you

That you may not want to hear

I will look at you with my eyes wide open

Grinning from ear to ear

When I finally say it to you

The truth will be so clear

You will not be confused

And laughing at what you hear.

**Reasons Why**

Ridiculous

Petty

And embarrassing

But, I started from the beginning

And followed through till the end

Underlying factors and reasons

I do feel them

Yet the truth has still not been said

**Fireproof**

It took them 43 days

Us –

I have lost count.

There has been no real progress

The ashes still smoldering and when poked set a flame.

They chose to do something about it

Stick it out

Regardless

In the end, hoping the true reward would be great enough.

And it was… for them.

You sit and wait

Dismiss things

You never took me seriously.

Hoping things would blow over

But, I'm on fire

Burning.

It's been a long time

Learn, adapt, and accept

Dare to love

Change

Balance.

Simplicity cannot embrace complexity, and vice versa.

Awkwardness shows and eyes cannot be penetrated.

But I now know

I am Fireproof

**Walk Away**

I throw him under a bus

He slaps me in the face

Incapable capability

A person can only take so much rejection

**Rotten**

Spoiled Brat

Fish out of water

You will grasp at whatever you can

For a reaction

The more I deal with you

The more I am disappointed in you

Ranting

Raving

Frustrating

But I'm thankful.

You may throw a fit

And make a scene

Drive me crazy

And make me scream

But you do deliver

And I'm sure you hate to

But it won't be long

You will see

The time will pass

The day will come

And we will be sad

When this is done

**Sing To Me**

Like an Asian Fused Diamond

Surrounded by

Fire and Ice

Love never dies

No matter the price

**Bring It**

Pick a fight

I choose not

Show your true colors

Mine are never hidden

Embarrass yourself

No thank you

Judge me

Go ahead

I am not afraid

You think you have me

Doubtful.

I will play your game

I will win

I never lose

I have strategy,

Reflexes, Patience, Tolerance and Diligence

I am emulous

You wanna do this? Let's go!

**Value**

It's not that I don't love you… I just ….

I need a different kind of love

My love for you is pure

And the love I think I need is jaded.

If I could just take a minute and enjoy

Relax

Appreciate

And consume the love you give

I would be intoxicated by the strength, the power and the purity that possess me

I see myself

Taking what you can give me

Appreciating the value and the beauty that make me feel unique and beautiful in your eyes

Not a Cinderella, Snow White or a Rapunzel

I can smell the Jasmine in my hair – I am Pocahontas, Mulan and Bell

I am a wide awake Sleeping Beauty

And the beauty I feel, within, is no doubt powerful and overwhelming

**That's All I Have To Say**

Where do we go from here?

That's all I have to say

I have no feelings, no sorrow, worries or regrets

No fear, no passion, no victory or success

I'm not beaten or broken or defeated

I'm not tired or rested

I will survive

Maybe not with my cup overflowing

But with knowledge and the ability to adapt to change

The flexibility and the experience to rely on myself

With love, and hopefully, patience from three blind mice

The seasons will change

And when it's colder this time

The mice will find warmth by the fire with their bellies full

Their spirits alive and running free

But what will you do?

Where will you go?

That's all I have to say

**Peaceful Nightmare**

Listening to sweet sounds

I kiss you goodnight

You are peaceful and unknowing

Drifting off to La-La-land

For selfish reasons - In a week your world will change

But, for now

A r o u n d

And

A r o u n d

It goes

Pivoting, Rotating

On its own axis

With you as its Sun, The Moon, and The Stars

My world,

My dream

So I'll let go and Breathe

**Thank you**

You are my leader, my lover and my class clown

Your eyes sparkle as you dance in the wind

What would I do without you?

The joy you bring me is indescribable

You make me laugh and smile with delight

I feel secure and strong when I am with you

Your hugs and kisses melt away any notion of a bad day

And fill my empty emotions

The world is a better place with you in it

And I am lucky you are mine

Why you choose me I will never know

But I am grateful

And I appreciate each day we have together

You call me "mommy"

And I call you my life.

Thank you.

**Happily Ever After?**

Our Happily Ever After remains to be seen

We keep each other at arms- length

Even though we have spent forever and a day together

We are still afraid of allowing ourselves to open up and embrace each other

Our Happily Ever After remains to be seen

We created a fairytale and destroyed a kingdom

Our princes and princess flourish

Our guard stands strong and the torment we cause ourselves and each other stands even stronger

Our Happily Ever After remains to be seen

Our intensions are pure and our motives noble

Can our hero slay the dragon

In our minds?

And rescue the damsel in our hearts?

Our Happily Ever After remains to be seen

**Same Confusion**

I don't spin the ring on my finger anymore

I don't check to see if it's still there

I don't marvel at its beauty or get blinded by its light

I do however miss its distraction, I miss its meaning

But I'm not sure I miss you

I do and then I don't

I actually miss our chaos, I miss the stress, and I miss the uncertainty

Yelling, crying

Being taken care of

I have tried to fill and furnish loves void with the same confusion

With the same stability that comes with disappointment

I always manage to have a decorated room

**The Blame Game**

I told myself I would never do this again

And here I am

Suffering, hating myself

Wondering why

Hating you for allowing me to do this

Again

I'm feeling like a drawn out, repeated, country song

Stephen, I thought you were my Romeo

But, you are driving slowly

And I am speeding down the highway

We are about to crash into Good- bye

I want this to be the last time

I sit alone

The moon is high

Casting red wine shadows

In my living room

What will I give?

Again….I gave

What have you given that you haven’t wanted to?

Why do you…I

Blame me…Us?

No one asked you to

You took that upon yourself, didn’t you?

I suppose I did too

**Five**

10 a.m.

Silence

Untamable restlessness

What would Noah say?

10 p.m.

All I can think of is the number

5

**Long weekend**

I am headed home

I always think of you when I am there

How nice

Maryland

How very nice

Not for me

I'm there for a very Long Island, 3 day weekend

**Forgiven But Not Forgotten**

Ball cap in hand

I should have been there

Sitting here shaking my head, I can't forget

I allowed the sabotage to happen

Knowing better, not even relying on faith

Although strange and inconceivable

Altogether unforgivable

I gave a lot that day

We shined as we collided through the breaking dawn

I am not a Carolina liar and I know when I am wrong

Strong

And although we have been waiting for this

I do know you're not ready

Jump in

Pockets full of sand

I tell myself

You're being a good man

AND Love lives on

**I**

I miss your good mornings

I miss your good nights

I miss our late night talks

The silent stir of the radio

I think about what if

And why I didn't

We had it all set up

The perfect plan

And then

I got distracted

I got distracted

By a voice that led me astray

And now here I am

Wanting and waiting

Desperately

Silently

To see your face again

**Back 2 You**

Every time I talk to you

I open up my chest and pour my heart out

It's such a relief but leaves me with great dissatisfaction

I am vulnerable

And the walls that you have built that protect you and guard your fortress are pretend

I can see through them

I understand the contradiction in your beliefs

I know you feel you are doing the right thing

You tell me to go

You continue to hold on

Pulling my heart strings

You are consistent and comfortable and don't want to be blamed

So I go wherever

But somehow I always come back to you

Like a summer set boomerang

**Flavoni**

Nervous

Excited

Scared

Disappointed

Voices held captive

Thoughts run wild

Silence - Question

Time ticks

Lovers sit and wait

**Guitar Strings**

The melody we hum has played for a while

It's smooth and strong and in unison

The chords you strum ache in my heart and relax my untamed soul

My mind plays tricks on me

I can't believe I'm the one

We both hate knowing we have been here before

Yet we want to share our experiences with each other

Knowing they would be better than before

Much more appreciated

We tremble, silk and satin leather and lace

Diamonds and pearls cannot replace

The confusion that we create within ourselves

**We**

I scream, I cry, I justify

You rant, you rave

You insinuate

The moment passes.

We are now dignified, we hope, we pray, we compensate

For our loss, we gain

Love remained

The demons pass, they cannot protest

All that remains to be seen

Is now- our destiny?

**Rhythmic**

Fresh lavender is on my finger tips

I can hear the roar of the surf outside my window

I feel its attraction pull me in every direction

A little mermaid, I will always be

Riding your wave

Our wave on wave

Watching your spotlight shine on me

Up the coast the light house signals

Your rollercoaster throws a tantrum

On wooden planks we can both move on

Together or not

However, I will, forever,

Sit here by the shore, relaxing

Smiling

Crying

Listening to the sound of tinkering rails against glass panes during your thunderstorm

**Surprised**

When I came up over the sand dune

I did not expect to see the lighthouse

I almost cried, because it caught me off guard

And I thought of you

**Thirsty**

She replaces him

Empty conquests and heart breaks

Immediate self-gratification

Heavy breathing

Empty beds

Wine

Tequila

And Screw Drivers

**Direction**

Different location

Same thoughts

A desire that grows more intense

A need to be fulfilled

A charade none the less

You're not lost

You just forgot where you were going

**It's Been A Tough Day**

The scribble on the page provides a constant reminder

I pull the covers over my head

And I put a cold mask on to tolerate the circles that darken me

My head aches and the room spins

A metal band sits alone on the floor

The symbolism is lost

And it's my fault?

There is still banging outside

But this time it's not you

The house is empty

Silent

And all I can hear is the sound of white noise

Crashing in my head

And I am sorry

**Untitled**

Thinking of you

Once again

Knowing we cannot, should not be together

It will be my heart which will be broken

**Welcome**

You were here

And you looked at me

Not once or twice

A question in your eye

Sip the sweet nectar

And let me

Plant a seed

Don’t be afraid

The unknown is exciting

And

Fulfilling

And if anything

All inviting

**Chameleon**

I think of you when I look at the stars

I make a wish

I wish we were still in high school

Would the conversations be less awkward?

And after we sit and visit

Would I wonder who you are?

Would I wonder if I ever really knew you?

Maybe you have never changed

Maybe you have remained the same

Maybe you are who and what

I want you to be

**The Devil In YOU**

Oh my God

What the hell

Am I passionate or possessed?

I was fine

And then

Who was that?

I'm confused, so confused

Is this all an illusion?

A charade

You bring out the devil in me

The worst in me

The death in me

The monstrous destruction in me

Yet again, I see it

You lead me to believe it's me

Against all better judgment

I allow you to

Bring out the crazy in me

I watch it happen

Again and again and again

I see my reflection and don't know who I am

A bull with plucked feathers

You shake your head

Point your finger, Judge me

But it is you

Who can't see?

**Day Dream**

I take your hand and follow you
Down the spiral stair case
Our warrior shouts,
“Be brave!”
Looking for a dream
I am led to a deserted room
To watch your fingers play
Late nights
And chatty talks
We smile, laugh and giggle
Forever?
Or just today?

**Poison**

I am very sane and sober

Yet the confusion and frustration still find their way in.

I witnessed a lot tonight

It was me?

But now I'm beginning to see

The poison and beast within

Escape you.

I don't know you.

I sat and watched the transformation

And almost allowed myself to get sucked in

Sure, the ending was the same as the ghostly past haunts us

Yet it was more controlled

Recognizable and Unwarranted

As always

I thought it made sense before

And the repeated so called defense demonstrated it once again

Made it more inevitable

Blame placed on each other

Misunderstanding curses us

Unfavorable attitudes and pride consume us

Responsibility misguided and we compete unrewarded

Trust, faith, strength, lost

What a disaster

Ridiculous ways to communicate

Unthankful apologizes, we finally agree

This is really not ok at all with me

**The Hand That Feeds You**

You were young and dumb

And bit the hand that fed you

Lack of confidence Or Lack of faith

Blame the world for you sorrows and disgrace

But don’t bite the hand that feeds you

You were held, allowed to laugh

Given grace and a place to show your face

And continued to bite the hand that feeds you

We were proud, showed substance

For all the world to see you

Yet you still bite the hand that feeds you

You were given a chance to see the light

Felt God dare you, ignite you

You missed out, Bailed out, Shouted out

And still bite the hand that feeds you

You bragged And searched And cursed

And you still bite the hand that feeds you

Sorry once again

And wondering why your plate is empty

You still bite the hand that feeds you

**Crazy Is Dead**

I can disengage and emotionally detach in a heartbeat

Good or bad - Better or worse

In the long run

Who really gets hurt?

I am beginning to tap into a power I am afraid of

One that you had seen from the beginning and as well and in fear of

You screamed

Don't Use Me, Don't Pass Me, Don't Leave Me

Guide me, Love me, Tell me what to Do

And then you call me crazy

So what should I do?

Well, let me remind you then

You can't rationalize with crazy

So, I put crazy to an end

And as for tonight I'm just doing to bed

However I do thank you for the lyrics in my head

Because once again crazy is dead

**Free**

I feel better

The house is lighter

Sage makes the room larger

Peppermint makes the air easier to breathe

Lavender helps the soul rest

Puts the mind at ease

No talk

No fuss

No confusion

We escaped it

Once again

This time

Now and hopefully forever

As crazy as it may seem

Love will set us free

**Who Cares?**

I heard you say,

“A face, that is still asleep, emerges from the coffin”

You would if you could, but you can’t, so you won’t

So predictable

So unfair and disappointing

I would if I could, and I can, so I do

But, who cares?

It doesn’t matter anyway

**Why**

She ruined a man today

She killed his spirit and watched him suffer

He had good intentions and only tried do what was right

He put up a good fight

He loved her

He loved her as if she were his own child

She rebelled and yelled

She went kicking and screaming

Warning him of the terror that was before him

He saw a flame in her - she blew it out

She was destructive with his heart and herself

Now they sit alone, sad

Mourning the one thing that was worth fighting for

Twisted and Jaded

Suffocating and confusing

Uncertain

Empty promises and resentment

Misplaced love and sharpened tongues

Spinning and spinning and spinning

Making themselves completely dizzy

It poisons and kills

And ruins a man

A good man- suffering then murdered

Viewed in amazement and for entertainment

The wall, now comes tumbling down

She sits alone - Silently crying

Screaming for help

Asking why

**Anxious For You**

Crickets chirp

And the house shivers with silence

Skin gets picked until fingers bleed

Teeth grind

As lips press and protrude as if to form an erupting volcano

Provoking thoughts about deleted messages swirl

Like a trapped tornado in open air

Forgotten moments surface

And an impractical shared request goes unnoticed

Torment smoothers sweet dreams

As teeth fall out

And the empty gaps make room to breath

**Loud Silence**

The broad axe falls upon the tavern tonight

Four screens are full of pirates who have

Thrown it away

Full glasses

Softs whispers

Empty messages

Last call

A gaze

A glimmer

I look away.

I sit alone

Within a room full of people

**Kissed Away**

The memory

The fragrance

The melody - I kissed them away

The chuckles between us

The paranoia around us - Kissed away

The insecurity we posses

The vibrations we caress - Kissed away

We are chicken

We duck

We knock

We drink

We call - We kissed the game away

We opinionate

We are proud

We stand our ground - We kissed it away

We appreciate

We deviate -

We kissed it all away

**Artificial Landscape**

I look to swim in the ocean

You climb small hills, not mountains

Play it safe

Stay comfortable

Test the water

Cause trouble

Appreciate the differences

Embrace the so called thunder

A kiss from heaven or hell

Cannot replace the challenges here now

**Loves Last Kiss**

You enter and declare,

"It's not over!"

The entourage in your head, cheers for you, screaming,
"*You're* excellent, *you're* beautiful",

Demanding - "How could she possibly kiss this away?"

"Don't kiss it away!"

Memories of incoming calls and empty blank stares,

Frustration of wasted, empty time, consume me

Of course I kissed away

Wait…

What did you say?

What am I doing? What is the score?

Whose face is that in mirror anyway?

My head is spinning. My heart is racing.

I don't even recognize myself anymore

Your persuasive influences reason with my doubt

While, P!nk's sobering whispers scream at me

And you now declare,

"Our love is blinding!"

Blow me… Loves Last Kiss

**Cat And Mouse**

We sit after a long day

Trying to relax And rest our minds

Unfortunately, we sit and think

Of where we are and where we are going

The seats around us revolve

People make small talk to feel comfortable

Ask us our deepest thoughts to feel a bond with someone….anyone

They make believe their life is worse or better than it actually seems

They are searching for something

Temptation or frustration

We give into it

Insecurity is usually the accelerator

Hence we – they – I enjoy a game of cat and mouse

Chasing our tails

Hoping that once we catch it

We can give it a gentle little nibble

And not bite it off

## LOL

I come to you, late at night, to lie down with you

Your fingertips glide along my arm

And my head rests gently on your chest

I wrap my arm around you firmly

Grasping your side as if I don't want to let go

I breathe you in and your heart beat echoes lively in my ear

Our eyes are closed

The voices from the TV keep our impatient minds company

We hardly say a word - the silence we share is comfortable

But, as the morning sun rises, restlessness settles in

I cradle your face as you ask –

"What do you think of me?"

And I laugh out loud

**Naked Twister**

So what are the chances of a guy like me

Playing checkers with a girl like you?

Naked Twister – maybe

Checkers – none

**Wish Upon A Star**

I sit in the dark and ponder a thought of mine

I look up at the stars as if I hear them

Guide me

Do I throw caution to the wind?

My decision making skills are not what they used to be

It would be nice

I stay still

Teasing

Wondering

Smiling

The time will come when we will be together again

And then what will the stars tell me to do then

## A Moment of Uncertainty

Wood separates the strum of his strings and the ink of her pen

But they do not sit in silence as they did with others in the past

Their intensions fill the air

He dances and prances

Turns about

She smiles and blushes

Sways in his doubt

They laugh and encourage each other to stay

**In Reach**

The rain has stopped and

I finally feel myself getting tired

I close my eyes, take a deep breath and

Smile

My body is numb

My thoughts are everywhere

The windows are open and

I hear “Good Bye’

Laughter fills the air

You are really something tonight

Ménage a` Trios, Glitter and Silk Touch bare skin

But you are there and

I am here

Carmen entertains you While I sit and

Wait

It isn’t fair. We danced in Chile.

Pretending its ok

So close, So far away, Maybe someday

**Windows To The Soul**

What are you looking for when you stare into my eyes like that?

I feel you are searching for something

Have you found it?

Do I let you go deep or only touch the surface?

Five seconds is a long time

Who turns away first; you or me?

I listen to your story and I feel your pain

Why? We wonder,

Yet, neither one of us can answer the question

What a tragedy.

Your body is relaxed. Your mind is sharp. Your words are reassuring.

When you stare into my eyes, what do you see?

Do you travel to a happy place?

Somewhere you can rest? Be free?

Like your words, are my eyes, reassuring - comfortable - enduring?

Are you waiting for an invitation to come clean?

St. Michelle still rests her pretty head

As the sun finds her way through the morning clouds

Not even one kettle has whistled yet, or has it?

It is still early

And the question still remains

The search continues.

I know what I see.

(For Bill)

**Weeping Willows**

That is sad

I think you used her to make me jealous

But that didn't work

And I think she used you to make me mad or think she had one up on me

But that didn't work

I think it's sad that you, my so-called- friend, hid something from me

This now makes you untrustworthy

I think it's sad that you lack confidence and do not respect others

Let alone yourself

I think it's sad that I am left here, alone, to clean up all this mess

While you call and ask if we are cool and she ignores me

I think it's sad that I have lost sleep over this nonsense

I finally put it to rest

Just in time for you to dig it back up again

I think it's sad that I am wasting precious time

Continuing to use my energy addressing this issue

I knew I should have just ignored it to begin with

I think it's sad that the two of you have pushed away someone who is true

I could have taken care of you and your hearts forever

How unfortunate

I think it's sad that you will never and probably have never had a friend like me

But, what makes me really sad

Is that you have no idea what you have done

And if you do, then my heart breaks knowing

You just don't care.

**The Surrender Game**

She could find someone who controlled none of her, but balanced her

But, as usual she is in the mood to use

And be used

She sends the distress signal to those that understand the rules

The enablers

And waits to see who responds

Logically

What if they all respond, “Yes” at the same time?

Then what?

The bridges get burned

The silver wear drawer emptied

A sponge

A punching bag

She tests the theory to see who holds the most truth

Her theory or his honor

The one she thinks will fail, responds,

“Yes”

Now she is the game

Honorable nobility

Afraid

She shouldn’t have

She cannot give him what he needs

And she will suffocate what he has to offer

The truth remains to be seen

He is a liar, she was played, and he is exiled

She now sits alone with a stranger

**You Make Me Whole**

There are some people that I just have a weakness for

You are one of them

Your smile-Your spirit-Your enthusiasm

Invite me

There are some people that I just have a weakness for

You are one of them

Your coolness – your calmness- your ability to see the light in the darkest day

There are some people that I just have a weakness for

You are one of them

Your love for your family- your openness and flexibility

There are some people that I just have a weakness for

You are one of them

Your ability to love me at hello- the way you see beauty through the beast

And your need to save me

There are some people I just have a weakness for

You are one of them

Your class- your elegance- - your gentleness

There are some people I just have a weakness for

You are one of them

You love me – haven’t left me- you forgive me- and you take care of me

There are some people I just have a weakness for

And though you may be different people,

I need each of you to make me whole.

**Two For One**

You slip a wine glass up her skirt

And a beer in his pocket - Why?

They both reacted with gratitude

Was it worth it?

**Because Of Me**

You did it again

Your smile

Your presence

Your fame

You did it again

You won her over, as you did

Her,

And her,

And her, and her, and her, and

Unfortunately her,

They sit, listen, and watch the two of you

Same words, same looks

Same frustration

She types

She talks

She hopes

She tries

She glares

They stare shyly

Then, they all pause

I walk in

The room stops

You smile

And everyone leaves

**Circumstantial Evidence**

Off and running like a beauty queen in a gay night club

You are like honey to bees

And your eyes shine a light of playfulness

The door is open

And although I am gay

You are gorgeous

It is evident that circumstances allow you to fit in anywhere.

**Mistress**

Wait a minute

I’m missing an earring

How could this be?

Call me

No, wait

Let it be

Good for him

Where could it be?

Between the seats

Let’s see

It’s out in the open

Plain as day

Small and sharp

Like a needle in a hay stake

This affair as well

Can no longer go unseen

**Crush**

I can't help but stare

I try to ignore you

Bite my lip and keep my head down

But you acknowledge me

Overwhelm me

Ignite me

And then, I blend into the crowd

I went to the powder room

Looked in the mirror and winked at myself

Thought I had a chance

Regrouped and held my breath

My heart stopped

You continued on

Did your own thing and interrupted me

I got lost

And you did what you had to do

I waited for you, cursed you and wanted you

Then, she left, we sat

This is not a good idea, and then I crushed you

**Fearless**

I hear you lurking outside

You want to drive me

Control me-Cater to a need

I will not oblige-Honesty protects me

I will use you as a catalyst to trust in myself

You will not win and again I will not let you in

Whether you like it or not

You will not consume me

Anxiety makes me- react impulsively

**Panic**

I could smell you

Soft and faint

You stood awfully close to me

Almost touching me

Trying not to blush

Playing it cool

Breaking a sweat

Oh my God, did I just say that?

This place

Conversations with underlying tones

Uneasiness about what may happen

I wish I had a manual to show me how to

"Attach and Attract A to Z"

You offer to help me

Assist me

And so I run

Not awaiting your response

I got scared – impatient- In need of

Immediate self-gratification

## Black Bird Fly

Dirty wine glasses still

Sit in the sink

Hiding a broken plate

The leaves whisper among the tree branches

As the sun peaks her head through the window

Black birds chirp as they open their wings

Freeing them

From the comfort of a cage that grounds them

## Probability

I keep running into you randomly

Unexpectedly

Our conversations engage me

And wet my appetite

Our time is too short and preoccupied

**Good Bye**

She finds the strength to step as the music holds her heart to move on

She closes her eyes

Takes a deep breath

She sits up, wiping the tears that bathe her

Sorrowful and alone

Unscrewed

Possessed with the yearning of love in her broken heart

Trying to piece together the puzzle that lies scattered among the floor

Dogs bark in the distance

And the motor hums as it exits

She catches her breath

Sighs of relief or defeat escape her

Her fists pound the earth and she holds on to her belief

Love will come again – Someday

**Random Thoughts Of Strangers**

"Elf hats and board games"

"Are you serious?  Are you serious?"

"True"

"You see what I'm saying?"

"He doesn't know anything"

"It's been like four weeks"

"He is a jerk"

"You know what I mean?"

"Dumb"

"Yo, whatever you guys."

"That going on back there is, Crazy"

**Bloody Wrists**

I don't understand

How could something like this happen?

It doesn't seem real. Is this real?

I am so confused

And sad

I am so sad

It's almost as if I am reading a script to a movie…or listening to a sick joke

What's the punch line?

Is this really going on right now?

**Untitled 2**

Planning fathers wedding anniversary

As mother sits crying

Remembering

They were married 50 years ago

And no one can tell her

**Said He**

Any time after 10 is good,

He said

I'm sorry for the other night

I was not prepared for what you told me

So Full of emotion and

I was shocked

I will see you later

For our heart to heart

I'm hanging by the pool today

Wishing you were here

**Waiting**

Where are you?

Thought it was an early night

The sun sets and people are coming and going

Yet your name hasn't been mentioned yet

Should I ask?

I do not dare

Free as a bird

Legs kicked up in the air

My fist rests against my head

No one walks through the door

Sigh of relief or frustration

But not real

This struggle is only an obsession

**Not My Conversation**

I'm sorry – what was the question?

It seems men handle business and pleasure better than women do

Hmmmm

After all these years of fighting for their right

They are still confused

Oooohhh really

Women handle family better than men

And men cringe at fighting for a family

Seriously?

There is and always will be a need for balance

Unfortunately we cannot find it now

But – wait- I'm sorry – what was the question?

I watch the two of you on the same page

Reading a different book

And it reminds me that what goes up must come down

**Parting Gift**

I didn't take home the usual parting gift today

But I left a few

I suppose it's something I have learned over time – to leave

I do however have other gifts I saved from your house but they hide from me

I am forcing myself to cry and mourn our loss

It's weird to think it's over when it truly hadn't even began

But it's time to get rid of the evidence and leave without a trace

With no temptations there are no frustrations

Tomorrow is a new day

OVER

**This Too Shall Pass**

The water rolls off my body like raindrops and hits the shower well

To me they look like teardrops vanishing into the white tile floor

Water pounds on my back and the sweet smell of my soap caresses me

Steam rises

And I think of you

I press my hands against the glass and bow my head

Breathing in the sorrow of yesterday

I close my eyes

Spread my arms out wide and press my fingers firmly against the wet walls

They are suction cups grounding me like a tree trunk

As the water erodes the foam under me

I stand in silence

Only listening to the voice in my head

Step out of the shower and into the light

This too shall pass

**The Score Is Tied**

My phone sits lifeless as I watch the clock

I eagerly anticipate a response

I interpret your silence as a no

My eye aches and I rub my palm against my brow massaging the pain away

I rest my head on my arm I wonder why I am still awake

I wait for that magical hour

You are alive

I begin to pace the floor

Occupying the time to even the score

Picking my skin until it bleeds, but even then I do not leave

I wait for time to tell me to go

And then I pretend there is no end to the masquerade we have played

**Mine**

I can hear my heart beating as I watch it trying to explode through my chest

The voices in my head scream and deaf tones ooze from my ears

I keep forgetting to breathe

And I think my lip is bleeding from biting it

My eyes drain muddy pools of water

And I have a frog in my throat

I have turned out each and every light in my house, as if, from the street, it does not exist

I roam aimlessly and wonder what to do with myself

Then I catch a glimpse of myself in the mirror and realize nothing at all has changed

Except, the grave I dig this time is a little deeper than the last

Grateful, I remembered to bring a ladder, so my heart is still mine

**Facets Of Time**

Chocolate covered strawberries tread water

Within the complicated metal

That imprisons us.

My eyes tip toe around sharp pronged icebergs

A good polish and cleaning cannot repair this trinket of hope and promise.

I put it away, so it can collect dust

Until, another day,

It is then, when its reflection will be solely mine.

**Doubted Decision**

They had a conversation today with closed eyes

Mixed emotions

Fears, doubts and truths

He should have hugged her

He can't believe he won't kiss her lips again

Or touch her body

He was strong and resilient, enough for both of them

She appreciates his honesty

Even though she wanted to, but didn't lead him on

He thinks, at good-bye, they both doubted their decision

But some things are necessary

He knew when she left he would crumble, squint and try to forget

**Rock A Bye Baby**

She cradled your head like a child as you share one pillow

Your arms are generously wrapped around her

You can feel her breath on your bare chest

You seem to be at peace - When you are at rest

As the moon caresses you

Your bodies move in unison

So not to disturb each other

When you awake, your strong hands carry her body

Into a new dimension

Your kisses flood her face and neck

You clasp hands as she bites down on you

I look away with one eye shut

As though asking for more

You pull her in ….And surrender.

**For MJ**

The tall grass turns its head towards me as I walk by

High Five

The trees whisper their cheers as I continue on

Proudly pounding pavement

Heart racing

Deep breaths

Sweat glistens on the bridge of my nose

One hour done- one to go

I accept my defeat for the day

Knowing fourteen more will bring me peace

And

Out of the darkness

**Me Myself and I**

I'm not alone or lonely

I enjoy me, myself and I

I have the world and you to invite me to explore

And I have a passion to investigate all around me

People intrigue me and their stores entice me

**Lost In Never Land**

I just started what I should have finished by now

What am I waiting for?

As if saying, I haven't even begun to begin

Time is on the clock and the second hand has no mercy on me

My skin is aging and my hair is graying

Yet my mind still stays in limbo

It has regressed and the goals I set forth to accomplish are lost

In Never Land

Fear still controls me and my poor fingernails show the proof

I must find the strength to accomplish the task at hand

Without distraction

But I am tired

Too young to be so tired

So do I take the taxi that just pulled up?

To Easy Street

Or will the ride only exhaust me in its own way

**Winged Demons**

We all have demons

Some of us hide from them

Some of us run from them

Some of us become a slave to them

I confront them

Most of the time- unexpectedly

Some of the time intentionally

Regardless, I pay the consequence

For the choices I make

Un-regrettable-ly I appreciate the lessons life teaches me

The people I meet through my journey are dear to me

I trust them and am thankful for them

Nothing is by accident

The chain of events leading to my so called defeat

Always ends up in glory

Because my demons have wings

My demons tease me – playfully entice me to do the things I want

Knowing that I will pay a price and I am not untouchable

Unfortunately,

The wings my demons bare confront me

Cradle me

Protect me

My demons with wings

Lead me into temptation to deliver me from evil

**Dream**

I have written this letter to you over and over again and have yet to mail it

I meet you in my dreams almost every night, because I have something to say

You walk in, always unannounced

Piercing blue eyes penetrate through me

I wonder what you are doing

I wonder who you are with

I wonder who she is

No one, you would say

"You're one of one "

But, who are we?

Status Quo, I suppose

Then what?

No thank you, I have been here before

I open my mouth, but words never come out

You look the same as the day you left

And my heart aches just the same

I want to reach for you

Hold you

But you remain an arm's length away

If I could just hold you again

Breathe you in

Feel your whiskers on my cheek

I know I would still be dreaming and realize

It’s time to cut the cord, wake up and move on

**Its 8:16 And Time Will Tell**

Silence rushes over the phone

As the call comes in over his radio

Loud and clear

She listens intently and thinks

For years, she has stayed up to talk to him

It's late and his family sleeps

While they share stories and laughs on their cell phones

She tries to imagine him, in his uniform, sitting in his car

Knowing, all too well, how other uniformed men look in theirs

Has anyone else been this close to him?

"Back in 15 minutes" he groans

She laughs- "I knew this would happen",

Another busy night, when I call

"Hold on", he says

Pause

Someone else is closer; they will take the call

They continue to laugh and share

Another call comes in

Advil and an 18 year old girl– attempted suicide - her parents were home

She catches her mind wandering and remembering

Mary Ellen

“45 minutes?” he reluctantly grumbles

He has to go now

He jokes; He is too old for this

3 generations and 26 years, is a lot

“Not much longer though”, he promises – “I won’t be doing this much longer”.

“Stupid people – poor stupid people”

She visualizes his head shaking in a disappointed manner

He tells her how nice it is to hear her voice

And hopes she will be around in an hour

If not, hopefully they can talk again soon

She smiles and wishes him well

Saddened he is gone, she thinks…

7 months and 45 minutes of conversation

She will probably never talk to him again.

**Forgive And Forget**

How can I be concerned or mad at you?

For not telling or confiding in me

When I did not in you

How can I hold you accountable for the truth?

When we all hold you accountable for keeping our secrets

How can I justify our friendship when the two of you have been friends

Forever

How can I dismiss protection with betrayal?

Regardless of what it is or was

We are all on the same journey

To find happily ever after

Even if it's just happily right now

**Southern Confusion**

I look at him like he needs rescuing

I am exhibiting the same behavior men show towards me

I think I just want to help him

But, he doesn't really need my help

He is fine

And I am fine

He has an aura about him

His smile lights up our hearts because it's not forced its genuine

He is nice and people like him

I like him

He makes me feel young and spirited and pretty

He thinks I'm sexy and looks at me like I am the only one in the world

He reminds me of me

Someone told me once, "We are attracted to those that remind us of us".

Southern hospitality is our true connection

So foreign, so confusing and intriguing to those who have never experienced it

**“I May Not Win Immediately,**

**But I Will Definitely Win” – Someone Said**

As I sit next to my so - called enemy

I graciously extend a hand of truths

There is no pause or second thought in my action

And the consequence remains anything but a mystery

The only outcome I could perceive is victory

“Keep your friends close and your enemies’ closer”, I have always been told

“And when your enemies become your friends,

And your friends become your enemies,

Bridges are not burnt but extended.”

And the joints stabilize, holding the structure firm and strong

Tall and unifying

One world, one belief in each other

In lay all lies

## BTW

By the way

I miss you

I have always missed you

Even when I was not trying not to miss you, but forget you

I missed you

I'm not treading water, but floating out here

I never tried to swim,

I'm waiting patiently for a wave to come

And wash me in

## SAT

You are to me

As I am to them

**For Rich**

Ten years

I let her hit my face

Ten years

I let her dictate my life

Ten years of kicking and screaming

Ten years of flinching

Compromising

Defeated

Ten years.

Two years later

Back again

Kicking and screaming

Two years later

Still the same

Ten years

Two years

Ten years

Crying, flinching, compromising

Two years later still the same

**Wanted Stalker**

I smelled you and I paused

I held my breath for a minute

And looked around

I closed my eyes and you were there

Damn you!

Stop following me!

How dare you!

But, thank you. I appreciate it.

**Get Out**

So – she *does* need saving

She needs and wants someone to give them a way out

He is distressed

He wants out. She wants out.

I know it

But, it really only confirms that she, he, I, we and they need rescuing

But, we are just too proud to say it

**My Hero**

Damsel in distress?

Strong willed, self-sufficient,

Needy victim,

Preyed upon,

Taken advantage of.

Heroic? Living spirit of hope.

In the end

Who saves the day?

How did,

Why did,

She welcome

Love?

**Flash back**

I thought of you the other day

And I realize, I am still waiting

I hate to say that

The feelings I had then;

I continue to have them now

Although, I suppress them

And chase them away

I know now, I wish to feel them

I know now, I wish to feel them

Why, why, why?

I thought of you the other day

**Just A Habit**

I do not think I had an effect, at all, that day

I just walked in.

I do not think I had an impact at all

But, you still noticed me

And I, you

An overwhelming curiosity of what, A habit?

A…what could or should have been habit

But, most things are.

People come and people go

And here we are

Right where we started

Evolution verses regression

We Are A Habit

Still practicing skills

That provide self-bliss

Overwhelming success

Nights filled with laughter

Fun and games

Musical Chairs around Poker Faces among us

Revolve - And here we are - The Same Habit

**All Lies**

I sit like a hermit

Trying to blend into the wall

People look at me,

Stare at me,

Assume.

I’m the neighborhood drunk at the bar

I mind my own business

And they request and require my story

Who I am,

What I am,

Why I am,

They fill in the blanks and question

Because they can.

I tell them and share with them

Nothing.

I create stories and lies

Just to entertain them

They seem satisfied

**Movie Star**

When we met I said," Hello Maverick"

You tilted your head

I laughed, as if you didn't know why

Collared white shirt

Mirrored aviators inside at night

Charisma and cocktails

A Tom Cruise smile

Unfortunately," now you're just somebody I used to know"

**Mission Abort**

I never touched her clothes

They still hang in the closet

The book I gave her still sits on the night stand

Decisions I have to make

I don't want to make

I am no Charles Lindbergh

I may ditch the plan

(For Norma)

**Not a Fair Weathered Friend**

A helicopter lands in the distance

As the sun sets

Its propellers vibrate the ground

And sends whispers through the tall grass

Waves shoot across the pool

As if a storm were rolling in

Laughter fills the air

And children run across the meadow

Cheers to our new found friendship

Not just a business arrangement, as others suspect

You roar a laugh as if it were you first

We smile and wine

Sitting and enjoying each other's company

Sharing a Cupcake or two

Our days and evenings are intoxicating

(For Paul)

**Insignificant**

Five down and two to go

Who are you waiting for?

Obviously, not the same person as me

So here she is

“Good for you”….” I think?”

No introductions and acknowledgement from either one of you

Nice

Isn’t that romantic

**The Doctors Perspective**

When I was 20 something I wish had seen the world through your eyes

I would have embraced our relationship more

If I have been more secure

At 20 something

I would not be so insecure and judgmental now

So, here I am.

Now, your age then

Seeing the world from your perspective

And the feelings I have are still those from my 20's

How is that so?

Proud and insecure

Someone looking for someone or something to hold on to

Never replacing my 'ifs', "maybes", and "has been"

And never fully establishing and embracing the foundations

To build upon

The perspective you wished to share with me then

**Today's Future is Tomorrow Past**

Why do I feel more comfortable starting in the middle?

Instead of the beginning

Is it more comforting?

Am I afraid of the beginning?

And why don't I ever finish what I started?

You would think it would be easy, since starting in the middle means

You are half way done

I was told once,

"That a single story can be deadly"

But, not finishing one kills me

**Hello Stranger**

So here we sit

Yet again

Time stands still here

Always comfortable in an

Uncomfortable way

Some players deal the cards

Same poker faces here stealing time

We wait for someone to make a move, as if

Surprised to see each other

A friendly smile and hello

Then awkwardness

Sitting seats away from each other

We cradle our thoughts

Giving each other an unspoken glimpse of yesterday, today and tomorrow

Afraid to look or acknowledge each other directly

Because, within minutes, we have become strangers

Tension and pressure consume us

Who will be the bigger person?

Who will apologize for the last time we met here?

And the embarrassment created at “hello”

Cards are revealed

Christmas bells ring and ice melts

“Hello, how are you”

Crickets chirp

Whose turn is it anyway?

**Sabotage**

I set myself

And

Us

Up for failure

**Drink**

I am here

You are next to me

Our breaths are loud and out of sink

You hold tight.

Snore and mumble

I take a deep breath

Toss and tumble

Breathing patterns mimic your tossing and turning

"Come closer to me"

I play dead

Lay still.

I then place soft kisses on your forehead

You grab ahold, hard

Pull me in tight

I bob and weave

Then I leave.

3 days go by

Should I have stayed?

Years later

Hard to believe

Our thoughts are still the same

Needing, Taking, Yearning

Needing, Taking, Yearning

Thirsty for you

Thirsty for more

Let's have a drink?

**Overflow**

I need a kid's cup

Something with a lid

To keep my emotions from staining my thoughts

**21**

21 days to form a habit

This is my first Sunday

And I hate it

Try again.

21 days to form a habit

This is my first Sunday

And I hate it

One more time

21 days to form a habit

This is once again my first Sunday

And I hate it

My first Sunday forming a new habit

Sitting alone

2 habits in one Sunday

I’m already failing at one habit

2 habits?

My first Sunday

And, I

Hate

It!

To Jersey?

His House?

Your Car?

Hmmmmm…

Let’s Run

I will start over on Sunday

**Give It Time**

I tried to give it time

But, I did not succeed

I question myself on a daily bases

Why?

I thought I did

I believed I did

But I lied to myself

I know I will be ok…

I hope

**Rebirth**

She sits at a traffic light

Closes her eyes and takes a deep breath

Through her exhale she watches the morning sun kiss the city

A flock of birds burst from the ground

They rush a power line and sit

Fluttering their wings gently

A surge of electricity jolts them into the air

The light changes green and she steadies her resolve

One squeaky wheel at a time

Into the future

When she will be given a chance

To erase the past and rise from the fire

Like a Phoenix

(For Gg)

**Random Thoughts Of Strangers 2.0**

"I'm a professional,

Trust me.

You'll be happy."

"Yes, I'm almost done

Ha, ha, ha."

"Thank you,

I would love some water."

"Excuse me?

You know what?

I'm sorry."

"That's ok."

**Fireball**

Mother Nature woke me up in the middle of the night

I could feel her wrath pounding against my window

Pain

She howled with fury

And the sound she made when she moved through trees sounded like

The ocean crashing down on a ship

Breaking it into splinters

Sending the crew to meet their doom

I listened to her

I felt her take every ounce of my sorrow

And transform it into rolling thunder

An alarm sounded in the distance

She woke you up too

Flames broke out

And the fireball consumed the building between us

I lay silent and smiling

Thanking her

For I chose to play peace maker

Today

Even though I am a skeleton

Holding on to the key

Of my heart

She defended and reclaimed my honor

I am glad Mother Nature did not call upon her sister tonight

For who knows what would have gone up in smoke then

(For My Sister)

**Win Win**

I broke my own spirit

Before someone else could

I thought it would be less painful

But it wasn't

The feelings and emotions are still the same

There is a rawness that exists

And an after- taste that is repulsive

I count the days and the hole in my heart reopens

I have to literally talk myself out of thinking about you

Knowing that the decision was mine

That I did right by both of us

This should be my prize

So why do I feel like the loser

When it's you?

Your trivial pursuit will not end well

Trust me

It's called experience

Yet, I know it's something you have to do

But, be prepared to accept the choices you have made

No one will ever like you "a lot" like I do.

**The Dish**

I wish I were confident enough to get my way

Speak my mind and "not know my place"

You think you know me

I don't care

Spit in my food, I will eat it anyway.

**Appetite For Pleasure**

I have a red door

And as I flip flop past it, I see the moon's skeleton

Dancing upon it

I soon slink past your barren beaten path and

Smell freshness

The tastes within these walls are exotic and quench my thirst

As my heart pounds

My soul vibrates

Waiting for you to get home

**I Miss You**

I miss you

I miss the sound of your voice

Your smile

Your laugh

I miss your gestures and exaggerated mannerisms

Your friendly disposition

And your sarcasm

I miss burrowing my head under your arm

I miss your kisses

Your smell

But, I do not miss the

Confusion, the drama, and the what if's

**Pick NO**

When faced with a yes or no question
I always pick "no"
It's easier that way
I wish him luck, though
I think I just got him to blush
"Yes you, damn you!
I love you,
I need you and
I want you to come over now"
"If I could, I would, but I can't".
You say, "So you won't"
Kids, school
Church, work and home
When faced with a yes or no question
I always pick "no"
It's easier that way
I'm not being
Difficult

**Demon Warrior**

Today, I found the first gift you gave me

It is red and black

Made of yarn

"A little something you can carry with you", you said.

"To protect you"

And I did that for the longest time

I carried it with me

But found that the little demon warrior could not protect me from myself

Or, for that matter, from you

So, I hid him away

Only to find him unexpectedly

And I felt a smile come across my face

"A good friend" was your response when I shared my find with you

Sometimes good friends cause a lot of trouble

Even when they are trying to protect us

And sometimes we are our own worst enemies

**Reflection**

You wanted honesty

I gave you honesty

And sometimes the truth is ugly

I understand your position and your feelings

I cannot change what has happened

But you are correct; I can make a change for a better future

And I would rather go it alone

I want you to be happy

Free

And explore other options

Because, I am not capable

Of giving you what you need or deserve

This doesn’t make me a bad person

It just makes me an honest one

And the truth hurts

**A Song For You**

If I could write a love song, I would write one for you

I would tell you how in love I am with you

How I smile when I think of you

How insecure, yet positive and comfortable I am with your love

I would write a song that screams how much I think of you everyday

How I would do anything for you and my every move and motive revolves around you

I surely hope to meet you someday

**It's Just A Tuesday**

Why does the universe keep throwing you in my path?

What does it have planned for us?

Are the intentions motivational, inspirational, controversial, spiritual or questionable?

You are very recognizable

A little indescribable

But I'm not uncomfortable

So why do I freeze and stumble

Act insecure and mumble

I think your feigned confidence balances my so called fear

Or are we reflecting each other's images in this broad mirror,

On this atypical Tuesday night

**Cloak And Dagger**

So - I had a lot to say before I got here

Now I just sit and stare

Hoping my thoughts would somehow converge and actually form sentences, so I can say what is on my mind

Unfortunately, I am zombie-like and forget exactly why it is that I came here

I know I had something important to say

I thought I had some feelings to express and revelations to confess

But instead I'm drawing a blank

And nothing is clear

Oh wait, I remember now

You, threw your dagger and denied the truth

When all you had to do was admit it, and say "yes"

Does your girlfriend know who you really are under that cloak?

Does she know she is a shadow and a doubt?

Does she know she is a joke?

**Conjure Up**

My heart aches for you.

I know we can't be together

It saddens me that we haven't given ourselves a chance to get to know each other, as each other

Our whole relationship has been based on a fairytale, which we have created in our heads, about each other or someone else we desire

We have only spent two nights, together in four years, and I have only kissed your lips a handful of times

Whose reality is this?

Will we wake up from this dream, full of strangers, to find ourselves staring alone in a mirror?

**I Gave Myself To You**

Whatever you gotta do to make yourself feel better

Remember this-

He wanted to be with me.

I totally wanted to be with you.

I only wanted to be with you.

I gave myself to you –

I should have seen it coming….and I did.

I saw it at "hello", but I still allowed myself to believe in you

I saw hope and I would not deny myself of love, but I beg you, please do not contact me again.

For I cannot bear the strings of my heart to be played upon

But, I did love you.

And even though I couldn't say it,

"You could see my eyes glow in the dark"

And I allowed you to do so

But I could never, and should never, have tried to compete with a ghost

**I'm Listening**

I feel their eyes penetrate me and their whispers echo my name

They ask random questions trying to figure out who I am, where I come from and why my awkwardness confuses them.

I hear I am weird or eccentric

I hear I am inviting, engaging, pleasant and special

Most likely just threatening

The weight of their stares encompass me

They try to possess me, provoke me

I am not interested

They want to look at me, talk to me, and touch me

I disengage, back away and RSVP, "no thank you".

Can't a girl sit and have a glass of wine by herself?

I laugh and say, "Maybe in 10 years."

**If**

What would happen if we were just honest?

If we spent a week together

If we laughed all day

If we fought like cats and dogs

If we actually had an uninterrupted conversation over dinner

I think I have only seen you eat once

Steamed shrimp

If we sat in silence and had a staring contest

If I served you breakfast in bed

But I don’t even know how you like your eggs

**Special**

Ever since I was a little girl people have told me how special I am

I remember it made me smile and blush

As I grew older, men also told me how special I am. This made me throw up

Today is my 39th birthday and I received a message

“We will never forget how special you are”, this too made me smile and blush

I met a man two years ago, and I cringed when he told me I was special.

I swore I would never see him again, if he should say that to me.

Because when men say that, they mean it, through their lies.

I broke a man’s heart last night because he said he has never met anyone like me before…

That I was special

I hate this word, SPECIAL, I curse this word SPECIAL

Yet, I embrace it when I see it in others

**Occab**

Pearls fall against pink lace

Glares come from a corner

Giggles make me sick to my stomach

Yet I smile

-Breathe-

The game begins and I am not sure who I can trust

But, I am confident.

As I sit here, I feel I should stalk the place like a hunter

Ready to kill my prey

But, I sit and chose to play the victim

With wet lips I indulge in the luxuries set before me

My senses fade but my intuition intensifies – protecting me

My belly rumbles, consuming fear and my face transforms

Desire intensifies, confidence builds

I am silent.

No longer afraid

Focused, Ready to pounce, Devoted to myself

And then, I Hiiisssss

VINCE
THEATRE

**Reminisce**

My spirit wants to chase you

My heart wants consume you

My head wants delete you

God, I love you

I spend all day looking for you

Feeling you

Hearing things that remind me of you

You haunt me continuously

Invite me

Taunt me

Where are you?

Who are you?

**Re - spect**

I have spent more time talking to you than anyone

I lay my heart down on a chopping block each time

My guard is down and your voice is like truth serum

I have expressed more to you, about who I am and how I feel, then, I have even to my best friend

I have mislead everyone I can think of

I am so tired of doing that

It's exhausting

I don't want that

It's been decided.

From now on I will give myself to someone I don't have to lie for

**Want Not, Waste Not**

I want to hug

I want to kiss

I want to swim

I want to dive

I want to see you

Smell you, Feel you

I want to engage, embrace, entice, seduce

I want to justify, not modify my intentions

I want to nuzzle your nose

And lick your teeth

Wrap your arm around me and tickle your chest

Stick my tongue in your belly button

And hear your laugh among a sigh

I want to suck on your neck

And tease your nipple

Let my pinkie wander and delight

You're young and beautiful

Naïve and smart

Full of vigor, energy and enthusiasm

Spirit

You remind me of me, and reflect an imagine I possess-

Possessed

Maybe it is the law of attraction or the way opposites attract –

None- the –less

**Drunk**

It never ends well for the one drinking wine

Secrets are divulged

History is debated

And the future still remains to be seen

With each glass classified information

Is laid out on the table

Then pointed to with blame

Wine is like truth serum

A massage

A resort that keeps feeding you grapes

It tans you like sarcasm

Relaxes you

Calls to you

"Open me"

"Twist me"

"Pour me"

Pass out

**Bent Arm Redemption**

All day long everyday

I am bumped and bruised

People lean on me

Throw money at me

Put their heads on me

I am subjected to extreme temperatures

The sour smells I encounter are overwhelming

The local teams gather and enjoy an import or two

Jack mussels Tom into inviting Mary and a few

He said, she said "What's that?"

"Do you remember when?"

My buddy Joe plays a song or two

His bent arm redeems Kendall and her crew

People love me

They call me "home"

A Royal Bitch asks for Sam

And Stella, the fiery red head, says,

"I gotta go!" "I'm done!" "Last Call!"

The End

*Circa 12~23*

***Thank you to my husband for being My One True Love***

***May our life together be nothing like the life we each left behind***